Blessed Marie-Rose Library
Christ the King School
12 Lennox Ave.
Winnipeg, Manitoba
R2M 1A6

Explore and Draw

Knights & Castles

Ann Becker

© 2010 Rourke Publishing LLC

All rights reserved. No part of this book may be reproduced or utilized in any form or by any means, electronic or mechanical including photocopying, recording, or by any information storage and retrieval system without permission in writing from the publisher.

www.rourkepublishing.com

Editor: Penny Dowdy
Art Direction: Tarang Saggar (Q2AMedia)
Designers: Shruti Aggarwal, Balam Singh Ghughtyal (Q2AMedia)
Picture researcher: Farheen Aadil (Q2AMedia)
Picture credits:
t=top b=bottom c=centre l=left r=right

Cover: Bradleym/Istockphoto, Matt Trommer/Shutterstock.
Insides: Snowhill/Fotolia: 6, Hulton Archive/Getty Images: 7, The Gallery Collection/Corbis: 10, Fred de Noyelle/Godong/Corbis: 11, Angelo Hornak/Corbis: 14, Carsten Reisinger/Shutterstock: 15,
Alinari Archives/Corbis: 18, Vaggelis/Dreamstime: 19.
Q2AMedia Art Bank: Title Page, 4, 5, 8, 9, 12, 13, 16, 17, 20, 21.

Library of Congress Cataloging-in-Publication Data
Becker, Ann, 1965 Oct. 6-
Knights and castles : explore and draw / Ann Becker.
p. cm. – (Explore and draw)
Includes index.
ISBN 978-1-60694-351-9 (hard cover)
ISBN 978-1-60694-835-4 (soft cover)
1. Knights and knighthood in art–Juvenile literature. 2. Castles in art–Juvenile literature.
3. Drawing–Technique–Juvenile literature. I. Title. II. Title: Explore and draw.
NC825.K54B43 2009
743.4–dc22
2009021613

Printed in the USA
CG/CG

www.rourkepublishing.com - rourke@rourkepublishing.com
Post Office Box 643328 Vero Beach, Florida 32964

Contents

Technique	**4**
Knights	**6**
Draw a Knight	**8**
Famous Knights	**10**
Draw King Arthur	**12**
Coat of Arms	**14**
Draw a Coat of Arms	**16**
Castles	**18**
Draw a Castle	**20**
Glossary	**22**
Index	**23**
Websites	**24**

Technique

Before you start drawing, let's talk about **focal point**. The focal point is the part of your drawing where you want a person's eye to look first. You can lead the viewer to the focal point in many ways.

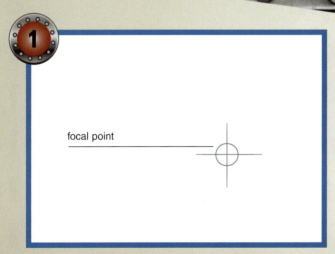

The focal point does not need to be in the center of the page.

Lines in the drawing can point in the direction of the focal point.

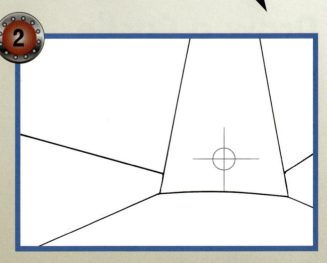

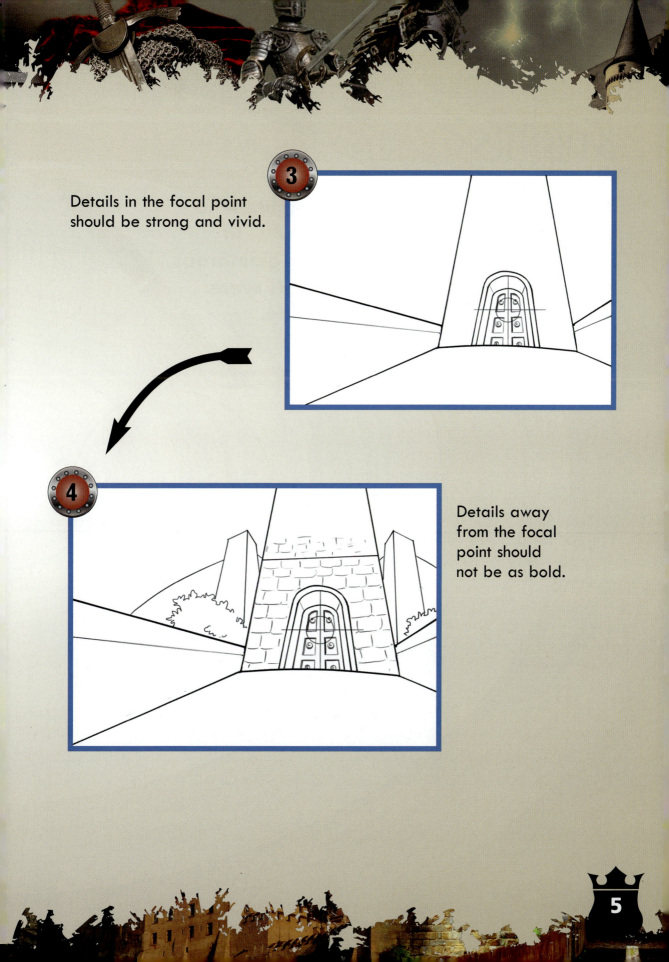

Knights

You've probably read about knights who slay dragons and rescue princesses. In reality a knight's life was not so glamorous. Yet for hundreds of years, knights were an important part of European life.

The Knight's Role

Rulers relied on their knights to protect the kingdom from attacks. The knights fought with skill and knew how to lead an army. For this service, rulers gave knights land, food, and money. The best knights became very rich this way! It wasn't an easy life, though. Some knights were away from their homes for months at a time, protecting their country.

A knight was responsible for protecting a king and the kingdom.

Becoming a Knight

It took many years of training and study to become a knight. At seven years old, a boy started living at the lord's castle as a page. He learned about weapons, music, writing, and other subjects. He became a squire at 14, and focused more on military **strategy**.

He also became an expert horseman. A knight on horseback was a powerful force on a battlefield! Finally, at 21, he would be knighted by the king or queen. Not all knights were male. For example, the Order of the Garter accepted female knights.

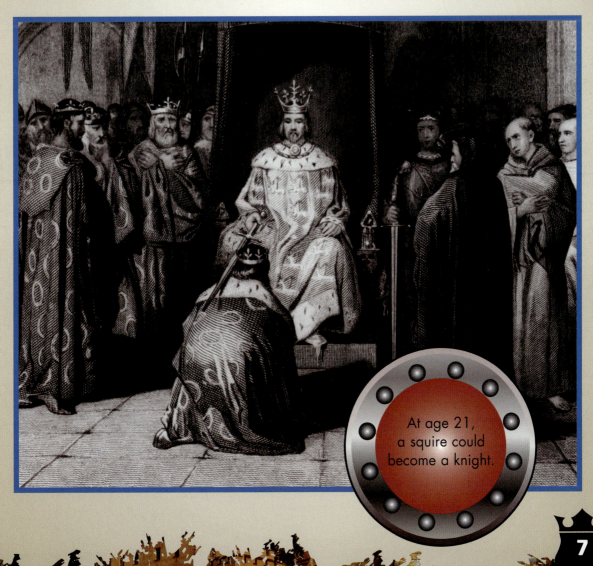

At age 21, a squire could become a knight.

Draw a Knight

We can draw a knight wearing a full suit or armor.

 In this picture, the knight will be standing in a doorway. The knight will be the focal point.

 The lines of the door frame the knight. Draw the simple lines of the knight's body.

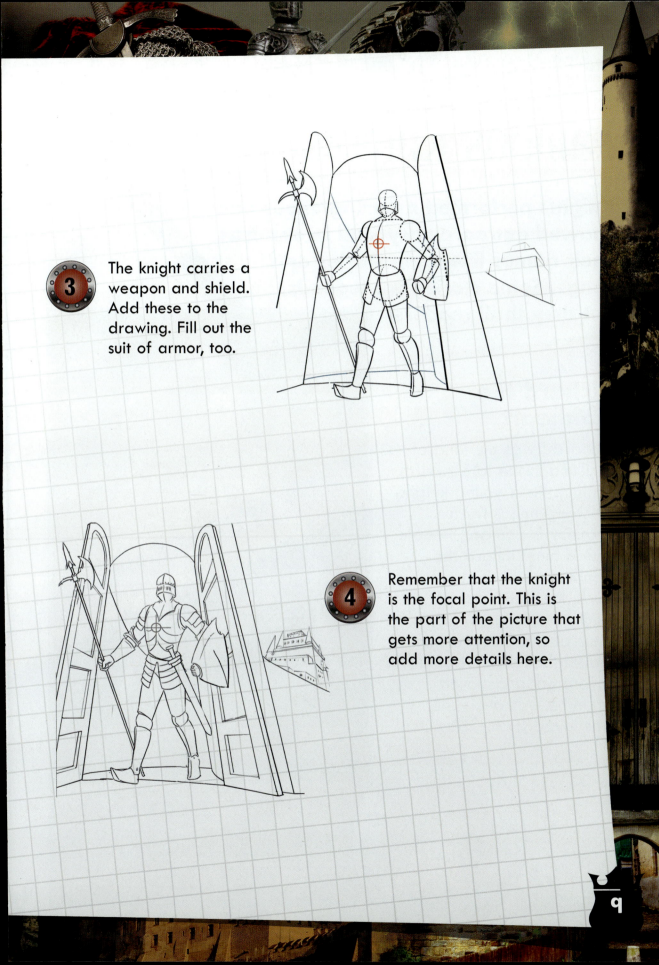

3 The knight carries a weapon and shield. Add these to the drawing. Fill out the suit of armor, too.

4 Remember that the knight is the focal point. This is the part of the picture that gets more attention, so add more details here.

Famous Knights

Knights performed amazing deeds and showed extraordinary skill in **combat**. Their names live on in stories and songs. Some stories are legends, but they thrill readers.

Richard the Lionheart

Richard I was the king of England in the late twelfth century. As a young knight, he was famous for his bravery in combat. People called him Richard the Lionheart and the name stuck. He didn't spend much time in his kingdom. Most of the time, he was leading knights in battle in foreign lands. Even when he was away, he was loved by his subjects.

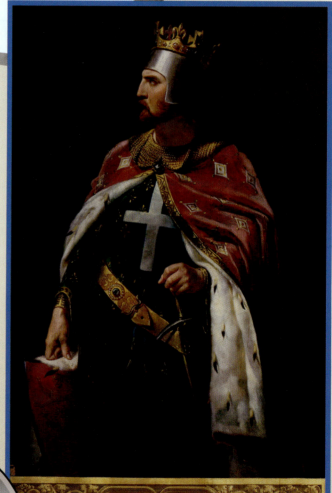

RICHARD 1er
(RICHARD CŒUR DE LION)
ROI D'ANGLETERRE.
+ 1199.

Richard I became king in the year 1183.

The Tale of King Arthur

Arthur was a fictional king of Britain in the sixth century. He invited the bravest knights to his court, where they followed a code of **chivalry**. One of his best knights, Sir Lancelot, rescued Queen Guinevere from Arthur's enemy.

Roland

Roland was the best of Emperor Charlemagne's knights. Some historians believe he lived in the late ninth century. He was known as a paladin—a special title given to only the best knights. He helped Charlemagne defend the empire, and he died in battle. The poem *Song of Roland* was written to remember his brave deeds and combat **prowess**.

King Arthur's court were called the Knights of the Round Table.

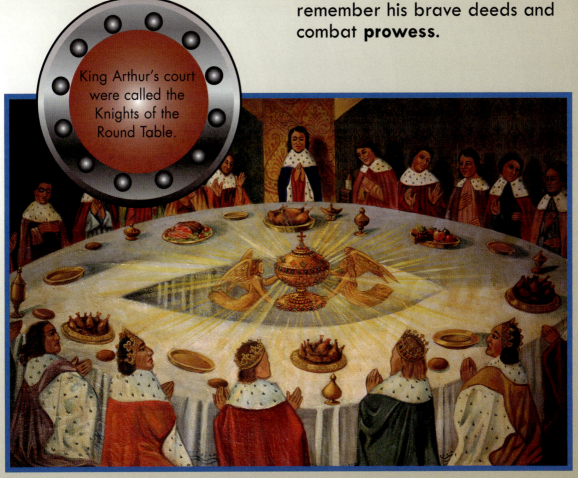

Draw King Arthur

King Arthur pulled a mythical sword out of a stone.

1 Place a few simple lines on the page to position the rock as well as King Arthur.

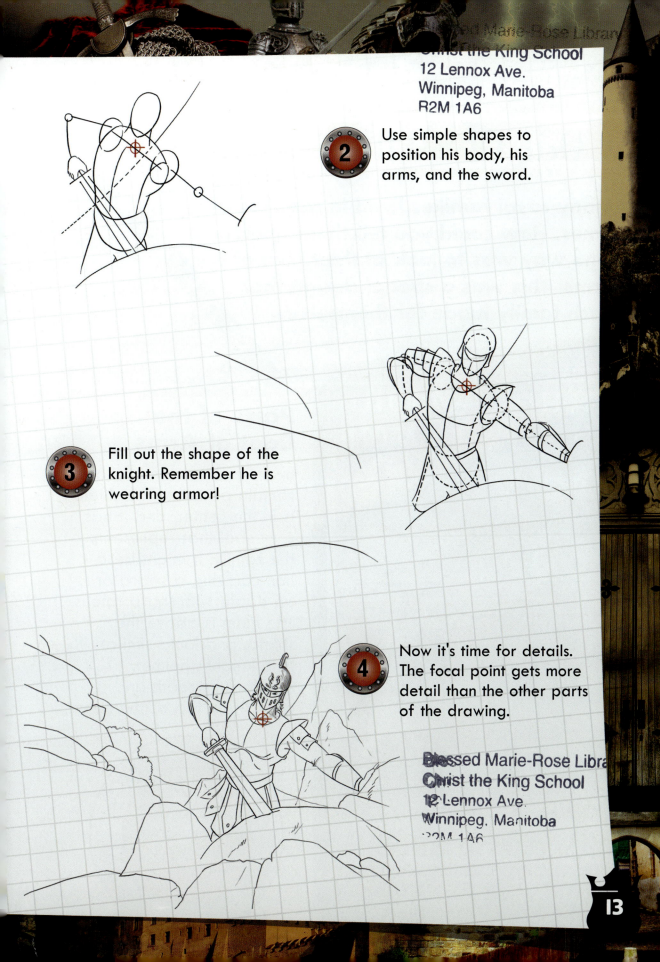

2 Use simple shapes to position his body, his arms, and the sword.

3 Fill out the shape of the knight. Remember he is wearing armor!

4 Now it's time for details. The focal point gets more detail than the other parts of the drawing.

Coat of Arms

Many royal families lived in **medieval** times. How could you tell them apart? One way was to look at their coat of arms. This was a special design that each family made for themselves.

Parts of the Coat of Arms

Every coat of arms followed certain patterns. The shield is in the center, and it has a symbol that represents the family. It might be a lion carrying a sword or an eagle with sharp talons. The helm is above the shield, and looks similar to a knight's helmet. A colorful wreath and a crest sit on top of the helm.

The Queen of England has her own coat of arms.

The Mantle

Finally, a cloth called a mantle is draped over the helmet and shield. The mantle might tell whether or not that person has been in combat. The parts of the coat of arms put together identify each family.

Blazon of Arms

The blazon of arms describes the coat of arms. For example, the field is the color of the shield, such as red or blue. A stripe across a shield is a bend. A charge is the picture on the shield. If a shield had three lions, then it would be charged with three lions. There are hundreds of terms in the blazon code.

Some coat of arms are placed on flags or armor.

Draw a Coat of Arms

Soldiers carried flags with the coat of arms displayed into battle.

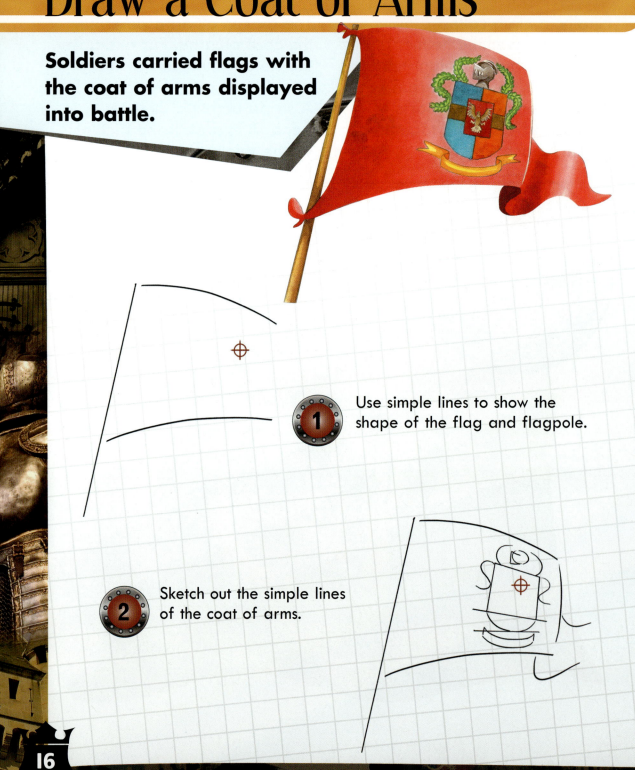

1. Use simple lines to show the shape of the flag and flagpole.

2. Sketch out the simple lines of the coat of arms.

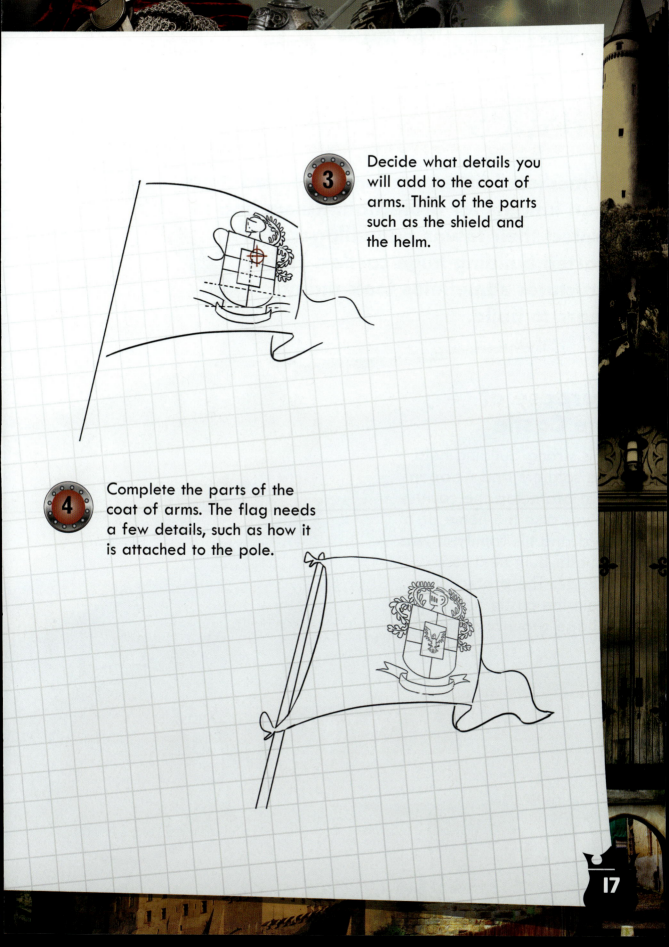

3 Decide what details you will add to the coat of arms. Think of the parts such as the shield and the helm.

4 Complete the parts of the coat of arms. The flag needs a few details, such as how it is attached to the pole.

Castles

In medieval times, a country needed more than knights for protection. Rulers had to protect their towns and villages. They started building huge castles. These structures sometimes took many years to build.

Purpose of the Castle

This strong building held the soldiers and weapons that protected the country. It was also the home of a lord and his family. It was usually built next to a village. The protection from the castle helped the village grow and prosper.

Tall towers let soldiers spot attackers from far away.

Parts of the Castle

People built many different kinds of castles, but they had similar features. The outside of a castle contained a huge wall with **battlements**. A castle had a keep, or a large tower where the lord and his family lived. Most castles had a drawbridge to enter from. All of these features made the castle easier to defend and kept the lord safe.

People in the Castle

People used the castle for more than just defense. It was a **vital** part of the village. Inside the castle walls, villagers traded goods and heard the news of the day. You could also find cooks, weavers, **blacksmiths**, and many others working inside the castle walls.

Water slowed attackers trying to raid the castle.

Draw a Castle

Castles come in many shapes and sizes. Be creative with your design!

1 Draw the simple lines that show where the castle sits on the hill.

2 This castle has many floors, so show how one floor sits on top of another.

3 Add the many towers and walls on the building. Show the mountains in the background, too.

4 Keep adding details. Castles need battlements and windows. Plants grow along the road.

5 Finally, focus on the fine details of the castle. Can you see how the lines and details highlight the focal point?

Glossary

battlements (BAT-uhl-muhnts): places in the walls of castles used to shoot through

blacksmiths (BLAK-smiths): workers who shape iron

chivalry (SHIV-uhl-ree): the way knights behave

combat (KOM-bat): battle

focal point (FOH-kuhl POINT): a place that draws attention or focus

medieval (mee-DEE-vuhl): related to the Middle Ages

prowess (PROU-iss): bravery in battle

strategy (STRAT-uh-jee): a careful plan for doing something

vital (VYE-tuhl): very important

Index

armor 8, 9, 13, 15

battlement(s) 19, 21

bend 15

blazon of arms 15

charge 15

chivalry 11

coat of arms 14, 15, 16, 17

drawbridge 19

field 15

focal point 4, 5, 8, 9, 13, 21

helm 14, 17

keep 19

King Arthur 11, 12, 13

mantle 15

Order of the Garter 7

page 7

Richard the Lionheart 10

Roland 11

shield 9, 14, 15, 17

squire 7

wreath 14

Websites

www.castles.org/
A website with detailed illustrations, photographs, and descriptions of castles from all around the world.

www.knightsandarmor.com
A website devoted to the life of knights in Medieval times.

www.kidsart.com/HotLnk.html
A website that gives links to art websites, supplies, and artists.

http://www.middle-ages.org.uk/middle-ages-knights.htm
A website which explores knights in the Middle Ages.

http://www.yourchildlearns.com/heraldrygame/index.html
A free online game that teaches about knights, shields, and heraldry.

About the Author
Ann Becker is an avid reader. Ann likes to read books, magazines, and even Internet articles. She hopes that someday she will get to go on a game show and put all of that reading to good use!

About the Illustrator
Maria Menon has been illustrating children's books for almost a decade. She loves making illustrations of animals, especially dragons and dinosaurs. She is fond of pets and has two dogs named Spot and Lara. When she is not busy illustrating, Maria spends her time watching animated movies.